Hand Book of Hotel and Resort Management

Author

Haidari Mohamed Benn

Vol. VI

Contents

Chapter 1

PREPARE COCKTAILS

Preparation of Training

Buffet preparation

Prepare cocktails

TLE: 4.2.1   Preparation of cocktails

Learning Objective:	The objective of this unit is after completing this chapter the trainee has mastered the preparation of; 1. Canapés 2. Sandwiches 3. Cocktail dishes.
Duration:	
Equipment /tools:	Slicing machine, knives, whisks, cutters bowls, cutting boards, piping bag and nozzles egg slicer can opener, trays, platters cocktail sticks, and gloves.
Training Materials:	Vegetables, eggs, charcuterie, oil, etc.
Instruction Aids:	Handouts
Reference Materials:	Practical Professional Cookery H. C. Cracnknell and Kanfamn.
Trainees Preparation:	Discuss with the trainee about; 1. Canapés 2. Sandwiches 3. Swahili cocktail dishes.

Buffet preparation
Prepare cocktails

Preparation of cocktails

Tell the trainees
1. What is Canapés?

2. Preparation of Canapés.

3. Different ingredients for making Canapés.

4. The art of sandwiches.

5. Preparation of sandwiches

6. Hot sandwiches

7. Club sandwiches

8. Bookmaker sandwich

9. Scandinavian sandwiches

10. Swahili dishes.

Buffet preparation

Prepare cocktails

Preparation of cocktails

Cocktail Parties

Cocktail come from the word cocktail drink, drink of which somebody can take between 18.00 hours and 22.00 hours in the evening, but there have to be some biting with that cocktail, and so the chefs do prepare small biting, small sandwiches, which are simple to take and put in the mouth without using a fork or knife, and without dirtying your hands or fingers.

There are two kinds of cocktail parties:
- International cocktail parties of which International cuisine is included.
- Local cocktail of the country parties that are practiced much in that culture.

International Cocktail Parties

These parties are ordered mostly by the Embassies or International Organizations or NGOs who will like to have:
- Canapés
- Sandwiches
- Savories
- Crudities
- Mini desserts
- Dip sauce

For example Swahili Cocktail Parties of which are practiced in East Africa will like to have:
- Sambusa
- Kachori
- Catless
- Pieces of cassava
- Banana tandori
- Mini chapati
- Chicken drums
- Fish fingers
- Fruit mishkaki
- Mini desserts
- Kebab
- Kachumbar
- Coconut chutney.

Kachori

CANAPÉS

The term Canapé generally refers to a shape of toasted or fried bread. Of a certain size and covered with game farce they accompany roast game birds; they are used to garnish certain savory foods and the name is used to designate many of the savories which are served at the end of a meal. In this section of the chapter though, the term refers to what are popularly known as Cocktail Canapés. These take many forms, but usually consist of small shapes of buttered toast or plain savory biscuit, covered with a savory item of food which is then decorated appropriately and, more often than not, glazed with aspic jelly.

Cassava

These small savory items are designed to be served as appetizers for consumption before the commencement of a meal; they can also be served at cocktail parties and receptions or as part of a buffet reception. Canapés are not usually regarded as a course of the menu though they are sometimes served in rapiers as part of the Hors-d'oeuvre selection or when prepared in the 'de luxe' style, as single hors-d'oeuvre. They are always served cold.

The following points should be taken into consideration when making Canapés:
(a). They should be dainty and small enough to be consumed in at most two mouthfuls.

(b). Prepare them as near to requirements as possible. Dry tired-looking Canapés can mar the proceedings of a reception or spoil one's anticipation of the meal to follow.

(c). Ordinary butter is best for spreading on the toast but flavoured and coloured butter can be used where appropriate – these last are especially good for decorating.

(d). Any decoration must be tasteful and in keeping with the fillings. The result should be appetizing to the eye as well as the palate.

Preparation of Chapati

(e). The Canapé should be cut or fashioned in a variety of shapes mainly determined by the filling, e.g. an elongated triangle for a sardine, asparagus tips on a finger-shape, sliced egg on rounds, etc.

(f). The use of aspic jelly to finally glaze the canapés can be useful to improve the appearance and can help to keep them moist. However, the jelly should be of an excellent quality, it should not be of too thick a layer nor too firm in texture. In many cases freshly made canapés are better when served unglazed. Good sense and a critical eye are the best guides here.

(g). The garnishing and presentation of canapés with centre-pieces is at the discretion of the practitioner and naturally relates to the custom and standard of service offered by the establishment.

Various titles given to the service of canapés include:

Cocktail or Reception Canapés: These are served as a selection of at least ten different varieties of small shape and size. They are best if glazed with aspic jelly then arranged either in lines or symmetrically, on a folded napkin or tray paper on a suitable dish and garnished with sprigs of parsley.

Canapés Moscovite: This is a general term to denote a dish of canapés made for a special party at a reception before going in to dinner. They would be made of high-quality ingredients such as caviar, foie gars, Parma ham, smoked salmon, prawns, asparagus, quails' eggs and so on, freshly prepared and unglazed. A dish of salted almonds or Pommes Chips may be placed in the centre of the dish.

Canapés à la Russe: this is a general term to denote a service of canapés usually with a selection of other appropriate items such as bouchées with various fillings, sausage rolls, goujons, chipolatas, barquettes and tartlets with various fillings and other suitable items as listed later in this chapter under the heading of savories. These last items should be made in smaller sizes and some could be offered either hot or cold.

Salmon a la aneth also can be used in canapé (This is specialty of Åland islands)

Preparation of Canapés

There are two acceptable methods of making canapés, the first being for large-scale production and the second for producing more expensive items individually and to a higher standard.

Large scale production
(1). Slice a sandwich or tin loaf into 5mm slices and toast on both sides.

(2). Immediately lay them on top of each other, press to keep them flat then separate the slices and let them cool.

(3). When cold, spread the slices well with butter and place the chosen item on the toasted slices using one kind of ingredient on each slice; press lightly to ensure they are fixed to the butter.

(4). Decorate the tops tastefully and ensure that it is spaced between where the canapés will be cut, then place on a wire rack and refrigerate.

(5). Have ready sufficient cooling aspic jelly.

(6). Bring the canapés from the refrigerator, place the rack on a tray and glaze the slices of canapés with the jelly. Replace in the refrigerator to set.

(7). Trim the edge of the slices straight then cut them into different shapes not more than 3cm wide.

(8). Arrange the canapés neatly in lines or in a symmetrical fashion on a folded table napkin or dish paper on a dish.

(9). Garnish with picked parsley and keep in the refrigerator until required.

Individual production

(1). Toast 5mm slices of bread on both sides.

(2). Immediately lay the slices of toast on top of each other and press to keep them flat then separate the slices and let them cool.

(3). When cold, spread the slices with butter or flavored butter.

(4). Cut the toast with a knife or cutters into individual shapes and sizes just a little larger than above, e.g. ovals, rounds, oblongs, squares and triangles.

(5). Arrange the chosen item one each piece of toast ensuring that the shape and size is compatible.

(6). Place the decoration on top and pipe with flavored and colored savory butter to form an outline, in dots or motifs.

(7). Place the Canapés on a tray and refrigerate; do not allow getting damp.

(8). Arrange the Canapés on a folded or molded table napkin on a suitable tray to make a colorful and symmetrical display.

(9). Garnish with picked parsley and keep in the refrigerator until required for service.

NOTE:

These Canapé may be glazed with aspic jelly if desired.

Chapter 2

Suitable Items for Making Canapé

Any of the following items may be used alone or in any combinations as desired:

(a). Cream cheese; slices of cheese; purée of blue cheese.

(b). Slices of hard-boiled egg; sliced cooked egg yolk; quails' eggs.

(c). Anchovy fillets; caviar; salmon caviar; smoked cod roe; smoked fish including eel, herring, mackerel, salmon, sturgeon and trout; roll mops; brislings; sardines; prawns; lobster; shrimps; tuna fish.

(d). Foie grass; ham; jambon de Parme; liver paste; pressed beef; tongue; salami and other smoked sausages; pastrami; smoked turkey.

(e). Asparagus tips; green, red and yellow pimentos; mushrooms; radish; tomato.

(f). For decoration: capers; gherkin; olives; hard-boiled white of egg; sieved yolk of hard-boiled egg; peas; truffle; piped savory butter; mayonnaise and anchovy essence; picked parsley; pickled walnuts.

Additional items which can be used at a reception or finger buffet include the following:

Barquettes: small boat-shaped pastry cases baked and filled with scallions of fish, shellfish, poultry, mushrooms etc. in an appropriate sauce.

Bouchées: small puff pastry cases made in various shapes and filled with scallions of fish, poultry, mushrooms etc.

Carolines: small éclairs filled with a savory mixture and glazed with Sauce Chaud-froid.

Celery; small lengths of celery filled with creamed blue cheese and sprinkled with paprika.

Cornets; triangular slices of ham, tongue, smoked salmon etc., rolled cornet-shape and filled with a suitable savory purée or mousse.

Croquettes: finely chopped cooked egg, fish, shellfish, meat, poultry or game with mushroom, truffle etc. bound with an appropriate sauce, molded in various shapes, egg-and-crumbed and deep-fried.

Dartois: finger-shapes of puff pastry spread with a forcemeat with strips of the item used on top, then baked.

Goujons and Goujonettes: small strips of fish or chicken, egg-and-crumbed and deep-fried.

Petits Pâtés: very small patties made with puff pastry and meat, poultry or game fillings.

Quails' eggs: soft-or hard-boiled, placed in a tartlet or bouchée with a hot sauce, or dressed with aspic jelly.

Quichelettes: tartlets filled with a savory egg custard mixture together with cheese, bacon, ham, mushrooms etc. and baked.

Scampi: dipped in batter or coated with egg and breadcrumbs and deep-fried.

Tartlets: short pastry tartlet cases filled with a scallion or purée of egg, cheese, fish, shellfish, meat, poultry, game or vegetable in an appropriate sauce.

In addition to the above, many of the savories in the last section of this chapter are suitable as hot items. It is only necessary that they be prepared in smaller sizes of two to three mouthfuls each.

SANDSICHES

Sandwiches consist of two slices of buttered bread with a filling in between which can usefully be served at any time of the day or night. The word sandwich is also applied to other similar light snacks, some made with only one slice of bread in the form of an open sandwich while others can be made with three or even four slices of bread or toast as in a triple-decker sandwich. Sandwiches can be a dainty component of the afternoon tea, or substantial enough for a meal.

The combination of bread and fillings are countless and the opportunity for creating new ones unlimited, but in all cases some thought must be given to their preparation. The quality of ingredients, balance and preparation are just as important as for any other dish of food. The following details are intended as a guide only; it is left for the practitioner to interpret them as seen fit.

Bread

Many kinds of bread are suitable for making sandwiches. The following are the most commonly used:

(1). The sandwich or tin loaf, because of its square shape, is ideal for cutting across in slices or lengthways.

(2). French bread, such as the Baguette, can be sued for making more robust sandwiches by cutting it into thickest slices on the slant and filling the centre, or by cutting lengthways on one side and filling the opening.

Breakfast Buffet

(3). Rye bread is suitable for Scandinavian-style open sandwiches; it needs to be sliced fairly thickly in order to support the fillings.

Preparation of smoked salmon

(4). Brown bread of all kinds can be used for making sandwiches; indeed some fillings are more suited to brown bread than white, e.g. smoked salmon.

Cold smoked salmon sandwich on black bread (Åland delicious canapé)

Butter

Butter should be used in preference to any other fat for sandwiches unless specifically prohibited, such as when proscribed by religion or diet. Butter gives a certain richness of taste but also acts as a barrier to prevent moist fillings from making the bread soggy. It must be used at room temperature so as to spread easily, or it may be creamed but not too softly. The practice of extending butter by the addition of thin cream or milk or not recommended. Flavored butter such as mustard or garlic butter should not be used indiscriminately.

Fillings

There are several categories of fillings for sandwiches and they can be used in suitable combinations. The most popular fillings include:

Cheese: any kind that can be sliced or spread.

Fish: anchovy paste; caviar; crabmeat; sardine; salmon paste; tuna fish; smoked salmon; shrimp paste.

Crudities

Meat: roast beef; brisket of beef; corned beef; chicken; turkey; liver pâté; liver sausage; ham; roast pork; salami; Parma ham; ox-tongue; chicken pâté; pâté de foie.

Smoked Turkey breast

Eggs; sliced hard-boiled egg; sieved hard-boiled egg mixed with mayonnaise; scrambled egg.

Vegetable: avocado pear; cucumber; lettuce; tomato watercress; mustard and cress.

16

Fruit and nuts: apricots; bananas; dates; figs; pineapple; raisins; almonds; peanuts; walnuts:

Miscellaneous: honey; chutney; mixed pickle; various proprietary brands of thick sauce.

Soft fillings made as spreads or pâtés should be well-seasoned.

Mayonnaise and cream cheese can be used instead of butter in some kinds of sandwiches.

Seasonings

The usual seasonings for sandwiches are salt and pepper which should be added to all mixtures and added to sliced eggs, meat and vegetables which need them. Seasoning must be complete as people do not expect to have to open a sandwich to add anything further. Mustard of the appropriate kind may be used on sliced meats and pickles where appropriate.

Preparation of Sandwiches

Sandwiches should be made according to demand of the service ranging from dainty to the more substantial. The method used can be according to volume of sales, individually or in bulk.

Individual sandwiches

Cut two slices of the chosen bread approx. 3mm thick, spread evenly with butter; cover with the chosen filling which must completely cover the bread but not overlap, generous but not wasteful. Season if necessary, cover with the top slice, press to seal and cut as appropriate. According to the custom of the establishment, this means leaving the crusts on or removing them, then cutting in half diagonally.

Bulk preparation of sandwiches

These can be produced as the required number of individual sandwiches but the following method is more time-saving where very large numbers are called for.

Using a sandwich loaf cut off the top, two sides and one end crust, thus leaving one end and the bottom crust attached ,cut through the end crust down to the bottom but not right through. Using a long slicing knife, cut slices horizontally through the loaf using the end crust as a guard, piling the slices on top of each other on the top crust. Spread half of the total number of slices evenly with the prepared butter laying them out, place the filling on top arranging it near to the edges then butter-the remaining slices and invert each onto the filling and press together. Pile on the crust and trim the edges evenly. If for immediate use, cut into triangles, fingers or squares; for future use, wrap the loaf of sandwiches in a clean damp cloth or sheet of dampened greaseproof paper.

Rolled sandwiches

These are made by spreading a thin slice of buttered decussated bread with the required filling and rolling it up tightly; or an item such as an asparagus tip, small sardine or slice of smoked salmon can be rolled in a buttered slice of bread. To keep the shape, wrap fairly tightly and refrigerate; trim the ends before serving.

Swahili mishkaki

Pinwheel Sandwiches

These are made in the same way as rolled sandwiches using longer slices of bread to give a diameter of approx. 5cm; the roll is then cut into 5mm thick slices.

Ribbon Sandwiches

These are made by sandwiching alternate slices of white and brown bread with various colors and flavors of filings; after being refrigerated the block can be cut downwards into approximately 5mm thick slices.

Afternoon Tea Sandwiches

The traditional fillings are egg and cress, sliced peeled tomato, sliced peeled cucumber, salmon paste, sardine paste, purée of white of chicken. Remove the crusts, cut a pile or rounds into small squares or fingers and trim the corners or cut into triangles, placing sufficient of each variety on a dish on a dish paper and sprinkling with mustard and cress.

HOT SANDWICHES

This kind of sandwich is made with toast, or by making an ordinary round of sandwich with medium-sliced bread and toasting it in a sandwich toasting machine. Hot sandwiches can be made successfully as single or double-deckers; if made any higher they become unwieldy to serve and to eat. They should be made to order and served while still hot. It is helpful to serve the sandwich cut into quarters and the contents of each held in place with a cocktail stick. The following are given as examples of their type.

Club Sandwich

Toast two slices of bread and spread each with Mayonnaise (185). On one slice arrange leaves of lettuce, sliced tomato, sliced hard-boiled egg, slices of cooked chicken breast and season. Finish with two slices of grilled bacon and cover with the second slice of toast. Press firmly together, trim the crusts and cut into two diagonally. Serve hot on a dish paper on a flat dish garnished with picked parsley. Because of the thickness of the filling it is god practice to pin each of the halves with a cocktail stick.

Bookmaker's Sandwich

Cut two slices of bread lengthways from a sandwich loaf. Toast and spread with butter. Season a minute Steak (786) and grill it quickly on both sides. Place it one of the slices of toast, spread the steak with mustard and cover with the second slice of toast. Trim the crusts, cut into three pieces and reheat quickly. Serve on a dish paper on a flat dish garnished with picked parsley.

Cape Cod Sandwich

Toast two slices of bread and spread one side of each with the brown meat of a dressed crab. On one side, add flaked white crabmeat mixed with a little mayonnaise, sliced peeled tomato and sliced peeled avocado pear. Season these then cover with the top slice and serve as for Club Sandwich (1613)

Denver Sandwich

Toast two slices of bread and spread one side of each with liver pâté; add a 3mm-thick slice of grilled gammon and a small heap of sautéed onion. Cover with the top slice, reheat, cut into four and serve with a portion of coleslaw.

Tongue and Spinach Sandwich

Toast three slices of bread and spread with butter. Place sliced ox-tongue on the bottom slice and arrange some slices of hard-boiled egg on top. Cover with the centre slice which should be buttered on the sides. Spread it with buttered spinach and sliced hard-boiled egg and cover with the top slice.

Western Sandwich

Toast two slices of bread and spread one side of each with creamed horseradish. Cover the bottom slice with shredded lettuce, slices of roast beef, chopped pimento, pimento-stuffed olives and chopped walnuts. Cover with more roast beef then more shredded lettuce. Finish with the second slice of toast. Trim the crusts, cut into four, reheat and serve with a sauceboat of Guacamole (203).

Smørrebrød or Open Sandwiches

These Scandinavian specialties are fairly substantial sandwiches made with one slice of bread only and with many different toppings and decorations. Rye, whole meal, pumpernickel or Vienna bread can be used and should be cut into ¾ cm thick slices. The butter must be spread right across the bread and the topping arranged artistically and generously on top. The crusts are not removed.

Suitable fillings for open sandwiches can include:

Eggs: scrambled; slices or quarters of hard-boiled; sieved egg with mayonnaise; raw yolk.

Cheese: all kinds including sliced, grated and cream cheese.

Fish: anchovy; caviar; smoked eel; pickled and smoked herring; lobster; smoked mackerel; prawns; salmon – fresh, pickled and smoked; sardines; shrimps; sild.

Meat: bacon rashers; roast beef; brisket of beef; chicken; corned beef; ham; liver pâté; mortadella; roast pock;salami; tongue; turkey.

Vegetables: asparagus; cucumber; endive; lettuce; mushrooms; mustard and cress; onion rings; pimento; radish; spring onions; tomato; watercress.

Fruit: apple; grapes; mandarin and orange segments; pineapple; prunes.

Garnishes: capers; grated carrot; pickled red cabbage; chives; gherkin; grated horseradish; lemon quarters; potato salad; Russian salad; mayonnaise-based sauces; pickles.

Sambusa: or in English they call them samosa are small deep fried pasties containing spiced minced meat or vegetables, originated from India but very popular in Zanzibar.

Kachori: mashed potatoes spiced with tummeric and other spices binded by eggs and then deep fried just like meat balls.

Katlessi: or Cutless in English is mashed potatoes, which either mixed with minced or cooked and then fried or the mined meat or fish is put in the middle and then dipped in eggs and fried.

Banana tandoori: pieces of bananas mixed with tandoori spices and then fried and on the top of banana you put a piece of sliced filet of beef.

Mini chapati: is a whole-wheat unleavened bread like pancake in Zanzibar they call it "Mikate ya kusukuma".

Chapati ready or mikate ya kusukuma

Performance Criteria	Direct Performance	Assessment		
		I	II	III
The trainee was able to prepare hot, cold sandwich canapés and Swahili bites.	1. Select sandwich bread as indicated in the recipe.			
	2. Select specified fillings such as meat, chicken etc.			
	3. Clean, peel and slice recommended vegetables.			
	4. Slice bread as recommended.			
	5. Spread the filling and arrange on the storage tray.			
	6. Work from left to right hand.			
	7. Toast sandwich in salamander.			
	8. Place the products on service plate.			
	9. Arrange the products decoratively.			
	10. Clean workplace tools and equipment.			

Product Specification	Assessment		
	Acceptable	Need for the adjustment	Not Acceptable
1. Sandwich bread fresh with small cells.			
2. Sandwich spread well seasoned and spread evenly and without soaking bread.			
3. Filling thinly sliced.			
4. Fillings fresh and tasty.			
5. Sambusa well spiced.			
6. Kachori well colored.			
7. Fish fingers are fresh.			

ORAL QUESTIONS	WRITTEN QUESTIONS
Question the trainee at the time of performance according to the task. (i). Question about handling knife. (ii). Hygiene. (iii). Safety precaution.	1. Explain in your own words the term canapé. 2. Name the suitable items for preparation of canapé. 3. Write down the steps of preparing canapé.

Chapter 3

PREPARE AND DISPLAY BUFFETS

PREPARATION AND DISPLAYING OF BUFFETS

Buffet preparation and display

Preparation and displaying buffets

Objectives	The trainee should be able to prepare and display the buffet either marriage reception or any kind of reception ordered.
Duration	15 hrs
Equipment / tools	Dish warmers, plates flower verses food tongs, knives, chapping boards mirrors trays round and oval etc.
Training Materials	All prepared cold and dishes and desserts.
Teaching Aid	Handouts, the displayed buffets itself management video cassettes picture showing displayed dishes.
Reference Materials	French for Catering students John Grisbrooke TLE's Level I in soups, different wheat dishes, and fish dishes. Classical cooking the modern way by Kinton and Ceserani Professional cooking by Wayne Gisslen
Trainee Preparation:	Discuss with trainees; 1. Introduce the subject of buffet. 2. Discuss cold food presentation and buffet service. 3. Discuss arrangement of buffet and appearance. 4. Discuss cold platter presentation. 5. Discuss hot food presentation. 6. Garnishing how it is done (techniques). 7. Arrangement of food on platters or glass display. 8. Buffet display layout. 9. Sample display of foods on platter. 10. Demonstrate buffet display arrangement for a function.

Buffet preparation

Preparation and displaying buffet

Duration	Instruction Steps	Illustration

	1. Give the information the originality of buffet
	
	2. Composition
	  (i). Hors – d'oruvre
	  (ii). Main courses
	     • meat based
	     • fish based
	     • egg based
	     • vegetable based
	     • roti
	     • griallades
	     • cheese
	     • desert	

Buffet preparations

Preparation and displaying buffet

INTRODUCTION

Buffet

This term refers to a choice of foods offered to the guests as a refreshing snack. The number of hot and cold dishes depends upon the type of occasion. A buffet can consist of a variety of sandwiches, a platter of cold meat cuts, fruit cakes, pies, and pastries, but can also involve the ultimate in luxury in terms of both choice of foods and the finesse of their preparation. When planning a buffet menu, one begins with the hors d'oeuvre dishes, continues wit soup, then egg dishes, fish, and shellfish. Then come the various meat, poultry, and game dishes, accompanied by the appropriate salad and the menu is complete with sweet dishes, pastries, fruit, and the dessert.

An example of order of buffet as per course or serving

Composition of menu

All buffet menus should be composed as follows;

1. Hors-d'oeuvre-starters.
2. Soups
3. Egg dishes
4. Cold fish dishes
5. Salad starters
6. Rotis
7. Griallades
8. Buffet froid
9. Vegetables
10. Cheeses
11. Desserts
12. Fruits and salads

EXAMPLE OF MEAT BASED DISHES
Raw ham
Smoked ham
Liver pate
Homemade pate
Terrine

EXAMPLE OF FISH BASED DISHES
Caviar
Sea food
Cooked prawns
Oil sardines
Tuna fish bullion

EXAMPLE OF EGG BASED DISHES
Filled eggs
Boston eggs

VEGETABLE BASED DISHES
Russian salads
Salad nicoise
Avocado vinaigrette
Cucumber salad

ROTI
Chicken roti
Lamb roti

GRILLADES
Pork chops
Grilled entrecote
Blue cheese

DESERTS
Crème caramel
Ice cream
Pastry products

HORS-D'OEUVRE
Fall into three main categories:-
1. Vegetable and fruit based
2. Meat fish based and egg
3. Miscellaneous hors-d'oeuvre

BUFFET DISPLAYS
(a). Cold food display
(b). Hot food display

Points to adhere to when presenting a cold buffet

COLD FOOD PRESENTATION AND BUFFET SERVICE

The buffet is a popular and profitable form of food presentation in nearly every kind of food service operation across the country. There are at least three reasons for this popularity:

1. *Visual appeal*. An attractive presentation of foods has the effect of lavishness and ample quantity, and careful arrangement and garnish suggest quality as well.

2. *Efficiency*. The buffet allows the restaurant to serve a large number of people in a short time with relatively few service personnel.

3. *Adaptability*. Buffet service is adaptable to nearly every kind of food (except items which must be cooked to order, like broiled or deep-fried foods), and to all price ranges, occasions, restaurant styles, and local food customs

Buffet Arrangement and Appearance

The buffet's visual appeal is perhaps its greatest attraction for the customer. Eye appeal of food is always important, but perhaps nowhere more important than on a buffet, because it is the appearance that sells the food. A buffet is not just food service, it is food display.

Lavishness and abundance

Above all else, a buffet should look lavish and plentiful. The appearance of an abundance of food beautifully laid out is exciting and stimulating to the appetite. There are many ways to create this look.

1. Color. A variety of colors is vital on a buffet as it is on a single plate. Plan menus and garnish so that you have enough color on the table.

2. Height. Flat foods on flat trays on flat tables are uninteresting to the eye. A centerpiece is an important feature, giving height and focus to the buffet. Ice carvings, tallow sculptures, and floral or fruit displays are some possibilities. They should be on separate table behind the food table. Center pieces on individual platters also add height. Large food items such as large cheeses and whole roasts being carved at the table are also effective. Multilevel tables, when available, are used to good effect.

3. Full platters and bowls. Replenish items as they become depleted. A nearly empty bowl isn't as appetizing as a full one. Arrange platters so that they still have interest even when portion have been removed (more on this later).

4. Proper spacing. While you shouldn't crowd the items, don't spread them so far apart that the table looks half empty.

Simplicity

This sounds like a contradiction to "lavishness," but it's not. You need to strike a good balance between the two. Lavishness is not the same as clutter.

1. Overdesigned, over decorated food scares people from eating it. How many times have you heard someone say, "Oh, it's so pretty I don't want to touch it"? Even if they don't say it, they'll think it. Too much design detracts from the food. Sometimes the food is so over decorated that it no longer looks like food. This is completely defeating the purpose. The customer should at least be able to identify it.

2. Excessive garnish is quickly destroyed as customer take portions.

Orderliness

A buffet should look like it was planned, not like it just happened. Customers prefer food presentation that looks carefully done, not just thrown together.

1. Simple arrangements are much easier to keep neat and orderly than complicated designs.

2. Colors and shapes should look lively and varied, but make sure they go together and do not clash.

3. Keep the style consistent. If it's formal, then everything should be formal. If it's casual or rustic, then every part of the presentation should be casual or rustic. If it's a Mexican fiesta, don't include German sauerbraten just because your specialty happens to be sauerbraten. This is true not only of the food but of the dishes and serving pieces, too, don't use ornate silver serving pieces for a country theme, for example.

Menu and serving sequence

Practical reasons as well as visual appeal determine the order in which foods are arranged on the buffet. As far as possible, it is good to have items in the proper menu order (for example, appetizers first, main course afterward, desserts last) if only to avoid confusing the customers, who might otherwise wonder what the food is and how much they should take. But there are many reasons for changing the order. The following should be taken into account when arranging a buffet:

1. Hot foods are best served last. Otherwise they would cool off while the guests make other selections from the cold foods. Also, it is more effective, visually, to place the decorative cold platters first and the less attractive chafing dishes last.

2. The more expensive foods are usually placed after the less expensive items. This gives you some control of food cost, since the guests' plates will be nearly full of other attractive foods by the time they get to the costly items.

3. Sauces and dressings should be placed next to the items with which they are to be served. Otherwise the customer might not match them with the right foods.

4. A separate dessert table is often a good idea. It allows guests to make a separate trip for their desserts without interfering with the main serving line. It is also possible, if the menu is large, to have a separate appetizer table.

5. Plates, of course, must be the first items on the table. Silverware, napkins, and other items not needed until the guest sits down to eat, should be at the end of the buffet table or set in place on the dining tables.

Cold Platter Presentation

The cold platter is the mainstay of the buffet and offers the most opportunity for visual artistry. If also can be one of the most demanding forms of food presentation, particularly show platters, which require great precision, patience and a good artistic sense.

Cold platters can range from a simple tray of cold cuts to elaborate construction of pâtés, meats, poultry, or fish decorated with aspic, truffles, and vegetable flowers. In this chapter we have space only for a discussion of general guidelines that you can apply both to formal buffet and to simple cold food arrangements. To learn more detailed, complex techniques, you will have to depend on your instructors, on more advanced courses, and on on-the-job experience. But this section should help you take the foods available in whatever kitchen you find yourself working and produce an attractive, appetizing buffet.

Basic principles of platter presentation

1. The three elements of a buffet platter:
   (a). Centerpiece or gross pièce (gross pies). This may be an uncut portion of the main food item, such as a pâté or a cold roast, decorated and displayed whole. It may be separate but related item, such as a molded salmon mousse on a platter of poached slices of salmon in aspic. It may be something as simple as a bowl or *ravier* (an oval relish dish – pronounced rave – yet) of sauce or condiment. Or it may be strictly for decoration, such as a butter sculpture or a squash vase filled with vegetable flowers. Whether or not the grosse pièce is intended to be eaten, it should be made of edible materials.

   (b). The slices or serving portions of the main food item, arranged artistically.

   (c). The garnish, arranged artistically, in proportion to the cut slices.

2. The food should be easy to handle and serve, so that one portion can be removed without ruining the arrangement.

3. A simple design is best. Simple arrangements are easier to serve, are more appetizing than over worked food, and are more likely to be still attractive when they are half demolished by the guests. Simple arrangements may be the hardest to produce. Everything has to be perfect because there is less decoration to divide the attention.

4. Attractive platter presentation may be made on silver or other metals, on mirrors, china, plastic, wood, or on many other materials, as long as they are presentable and suitable for use with food. Metal platters that might cause discoloration or metallic flavors are often covered with a thin layer of aspic before the food is placed on them.

5. Once a piece of food has touched the tray, do not remove it. Shiny silver or mirror trays are easily smudged, and you'll have to wash the tray and start over again. This shows the importance of good preplanning. Following this rule also helps eliminate over-handling of food, which is a bad sanitary practice.

6. Think of the platter as part of the whole buffet. It must look attractive and appropriate not only by itself but among the other presentations on the table. The arrangement should always be planned from the same angle from which it will be seen on the buffet.

Designing the platter

1. *Plan ahead.* Making a sketch is a good idea. Otherwise you might have half the food on the platter and suddenly realize you have to start over because everything doesn't fit the way you had hoped. The result is wasted time and excessive handling of food. One way to start a sketch is to divide the platter into six or eight equal parts. This helps you avoid lopsided or crooked arrangements by giving you equally spaced markets to guide you. It is relatively easy, then to sketch in a balanced, symmetrical layout as the examples show.

2. ***Get movement into your design***

    This doesn't mean that you should mount the food on little wheels. It means that a good design makes your eyes move across the platter following the lines you have set up. Most food for platters consists of single small portions arranged in rows or lines. The trick is to put movement into those lines by curving or angling them.

HOT FOOD PRESENTATION

The Importance of Appearance

We eat for enjoyment as well as for nutrition and sustenance. Cooking is not just a trade but an art that appeals to our senses of taste, smell, and sight. "The eye east first" is a well-known maximum. Our first impressions of a plate of food set our expectations. The sight of food stimulated our appetites, starts our digestive juices flowing, and makes us eager to "dig in". Our meal becomes exciting and stimulating. On the other hand, if the food looks carelessly served, tossed onto the plate in a sloppy manner, we assume it was cooked with the same lack of care. If the colors are pale and washed out, with no color accent, we expect the flavors to be bland and monotonous. If the size of the plate makes the steak look small even it it's not), we go away unsatisfied. Your job as cooks and chefs then is to get your customers interested in your food or, better yet, excited about it. You can't afford to turn them off before they even taste it. Your success depends upon making your customers happy. Making food look good requires first of all that you use proper cooking techniques. If a fish is overcooked and dry or a green vegetable is drab and mushy, it won't look good no matter what you do with it. Second, serving attractive food is largely a matter of being neat and careful and using common sense.

Garden Buffet

Professionals take pride in their work and in the food they serve. They don't put up a plate with sauce dribbled all over the rim and may be a thumb print or two for extra effect not because their supervisors told them not to or because a rule in a textbook says "don't dribble sauce all over the rim of the plate," but because it's not professional.

Third, beyond just being neat, effective food presentation depends upon developing an understanding of techniques involving balance, arrangement, and garniture. These are the subjects of our next sections.

Fundamentals of Plating

We've said before that a plate of food is like a picture, and the rim of the plate is the frame. This does not mean that you have to spend as much time arranging the plate but it does mean that you think a little like an artist and strive for a pleasing arrangement.

One caution: Don't get carried away. A plate that's too elaborate can be as bad as one that's too careless. Besides, you want that hot dinner to be still hot when it reaches the customer, and you don't have time to get too fancy.

Display of garden buffet

Since most of this chapter is about the visual aspects of food, you will want to refer to the color photographs in this text as you read the general rules that follow. Even more important, you should pay close attention whenever you instructors demonstrate plating up food or arranging platters.

Balance

Balance is a term we used when talking about menu planning. The rules of good menu balance also apply to plating. Select foods and garnishes that offer variety and contrast, while at the same time avoiding combinations that are awkward or jarring.

Beach buffet scenario

Colors

Two or three colors on a plate are usually more interesting than just one. Visualize this combination: poached chicken breast with supreme sauce, mashed potatoes, and steamed cauliflower. Appetizing! or how about fried chicken, French fries, and corn? Not quite so bad, but still a little monotonous.

Many hot foods, especially meats, poultry, and fish, have little color other than shades of brown, gold, or white. It helps to select vegetables or accompaniments that add color interest – one reason why green vegetables are so popular.

Garnish is often unnecessary, especially if the accompaniments have color, but it is very important in some cases. The classic American combination of broiled steak (brown) and baked potato (brown and white) looks a little livelier with even the simple addition of a healthy sprig of watercress or parsley

1. Shapes

Plan for variety of shapes and forms as well as of colors, for example, you probably to do not want to serve Brussels sprouts with meatballs and new potatoes. Your customers might get up a game of marbles. Green beans and whipped potatoes might be better choices for accompaniments. Cutting vegetables into different shapes gives you great flexibility. Carrots, for examples, which can be cut into dice, rounds, or sticks (batonnet, julienne, etc), can be adapted to nearly any plate

2. Textures

Textures are not strictly visual considerations, but they are important in plating as in menu planning good balance requires a variety of textures on the plate. Perhaps the most common error is serving too many soft of purée foods, such as baked salmon loaf with whipped potatoes and puréed squash.

3. Flavors

You can't see flavors, either, but this is one more factor you must consider when balancing colors, shapes, and textures on the plate. Consult the menu planning guidelines.

Garnish

What is garnish?

The word "garnish" is derived from a French word meaning "to adorn or to furnish". In English, we use the word to mean to decorate or embellish a food item by the addition of other items. The word also is used for these decorative items.

This definition at first seems too vague, because it could include just about anything. But, in fact, the term has been used for a great variety of preparations and techniques in the history of classical and modern cuisine. Let's look at some of these styles of garnish and what they mean to today's cooks and chefs.

First, however, we'll briefly define some similar words that are often confused.

Garnish refers to decorative edible items used to ornament or to enhance the eye appeal of another food item.

To garnish means to add such a decorative item to food.

Garniture is the French word for garnish and means the same thing. Garniture also means "the act of process of garnishing".

Garni means "garnished". It does not refer to the decorative item but describes the main food item by stating that is has had garnish added to it. In other words, you say "steak garni" (garnished steak), not "steak with garni".

Classical garnish

In classical French cooking, the terms garnish and garniture have been used the way we use the term accompaniments. In other words, garnishes are any items placed on the platter or plate or in the soup bowl in addition to the main item. It happens that these accompaniments also make the food look more attractive, but that is not the emphasis.

The classical French chef had a tremendous repertory of simple and elaborate garnishes, and they all had specific names. A trained chef, or a well informed diner for that matter, knew that the word Rachel on the menu meant that the dish was served with artichoke bottoms filled with poached marrow and that Portuguese meant a garnish of stuffed tomatoes.

There were so many of these names, however, that no one could remember them all. So they were catalogued in handbooks for the use of chefs. *Le Répertoire de la Cuisine,* one of these handbooks, has 209 listings in the garnish section alone, not to mention nearly 7000 other preparations, all with their own names. The garnishes may be simple as the one called Concorde or as complex as the one called Tortue, quoted here to give you an idea of the complexity and elaborateness of classical garnish.

Dessert table

Concorde *(for large joints)* – Peas, glazed carrots, mashes potatoes
Tortue *(for Entées)* – Quenelles, mushroom heads, gherkins, garlic, collops of tongue and calves brains, small fried eggs, heart shapes croutons, crayfish, slices of truffles. Tartare sauce

Technique: Fried Parsley

1. Separate sprigs and remove coarse stems.
2. Wash. Dry thoroughly
3. Deep-fry for just a few seconds, until crisp but still green.
4. Drain on absorbent paper. Serve immediately.

Technique: Cucumbers

1. For decorative slices, score unpeeled cucumber with a fork or flute with a channel knife before slicing.
2. For twists, cut slices three fourths of the way across, twist open, and stand on plate.
3. For cups, cut fluted cucumber in one-inch section, hollow out slightly with a melon ball cutter or spoon, and fill with an appropriate condiment or sauce.

Cucumber garnishes can be made more decorative
By scoring the cucumber (a) with a fork

(b). with channel knife before slicing or cutting. See technique 2.

Chapter 4
Techniques for making garnishes for buffets

1. Fluting mushrooms is a technique that takes a great deal of practice to get the knack of. Follow the steps or watch your instructor demonstrate. Then, whenever you have to slice mushrooms, practice fluting a few. Eventually you'll get it.

2. To keep mushrooms white; simmer 2 to 3 minutes in salted water with a little butter and lemon juice.

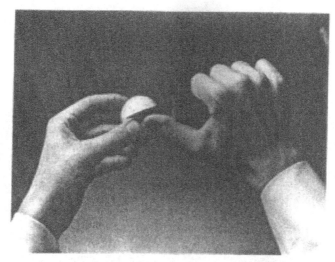

Fluting mushrooms (Technique 3).
(a) Holding the mushroom as shown, place the blade of a sharp paring knife at an angle against the cap of the mushroom, with the thumb of your knife hand resting on the mushroom and bracing the back of the knife.

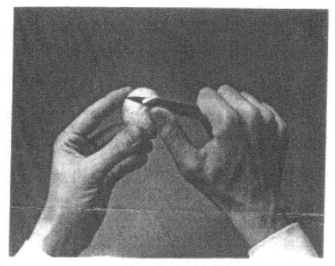

(b) Begin to rotate the knife, using your thumb as a pivot point. The knife should begin to cut a shallow groove from the mushroom.

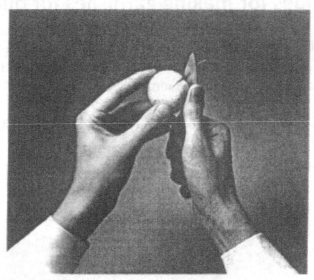

(c) Turn the knife until the groove extends over the edge of the cap as shown.

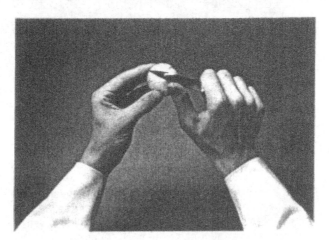

(d) Turn the mushroom a few degrees and repeat the action to make another groove next to the first one.

(e) Continue until the entire mushroom is fluted.

Technique 4 Radishes

1. Radishes can be cut in many ways to make decorative garnishes.
2. After cutting, soak the radishes in ice water until they open up.

 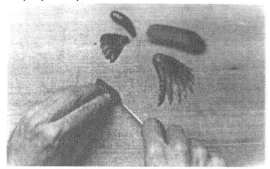

Radishes can be cut into many decorative (technique 6) may
Forms, including these shown here (technique 4) gherkins

Pickle fans

be cut from tiny or

From slices of large dill

Pickles

Technique 5 Scallion Brushes

1. Cut off the root ends of the scallions, including the little hard core. Cut the white part into 2-inch sections.

2. With a thin bladed knife, spilt both ends of the scallion pieces with cuts ½ inch deep. Make enough cuts to separate the ends into fine shreds,

3. Soak in cold water until the ends curl up.

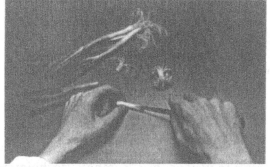 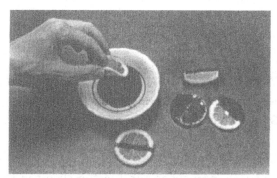

Scallions for garnish can be cut as described in Technique 5 slices and wedges may be

Lemon garnishes (Technique 7).
(a.)   lemon

Decorated with paprika or chopped

Parsley, peeled lemon slices may

(b.) *Simple lemon halves are made more decorative by cutting as showing*

(c). *This illustration shows another way of presenting lemon halves as garnish. After cutting the, the halves may be decorated with paprika parsley.*

Technique 6 Pickle Fans
1. With the stem end of the pickle away from you, make a series of thin vertical slices the length of the pickle but do not cut through the stem end
2. Spread the pickle into a fan shape as shown.

Technique 7 Lemons
1. Fluted lemon slices and twisted slice are cut the same way as for cucumbers (technique 2). Slices placed directly on fish or meat is cut from peeled lemons.

2. Dip half the slice in paprika or finely chopped parsley for a colorful effect. For just a line of paprika down the center, bend the slice between the fingers, as shown in the illustration, and dip lightly in paprika.

3. Wedges are often more attractive if the ends of the lemons are cut off first. For added color, dip the edge of the wedge in paprika as shown.

4. For lemon halves, first cut a thin slice from each end of the lemon so the halves will stand straight. Cut a long strip from the outer edge of the lemon half, but do not detach it. Tie a knot in the strip, being careful not to break it. Or you may cut two strips, one from either side, and make tow knots. Decorate with parsley.

5. For a saw tooth edge, cut the pattern, piercing all the way to the center of the lemon with the knife. Separate the two halves. Decorate with parsley, or dip the points of the teeth in paprika.

Technique 8 Frosted Grapes

1. Separate the grape into small bunches. Brush with lightly beaten egg white and sprinkle with granulated sugar.

2. Let dry before serving.

To prepare toast point, cut bread slices into triangles or heart shapes as shown. Fry the bread shapes in butter and dip in sauce and then in parsley.

Technique 9 Toast Points

1. Cut slices of Pullman bread in half diagonally. Trim the crust off and cut each piece into a heart shape as shown save the trimmings for breadcrumbs.

2. Sauté the pieces in butter and oil until golden on both sides.

3. Dip the tips into the sauce that is being served with the dish the toast points are to garnish, and then into chopped parsley.

Classical terms in the modern kitchen

Many of the classical names for garnishes are still used in American kitchens, although they have lost the precise meanings the once had. You will encounter these terms frequently, so it is worthwhile learning them.

Remember that the following definitions are not the classical ones, but simply the garnishes are accompaniment generally indicated by the terms in today's kitchens.

Bouquetière: "bouquet" of vegetables
Jardinière: "garden" vegetables
Printanière: spring vegetables
Primeurs: first spring vegetables
These four terms refer to assortments of fresh vegetables, including carrots, turnips, peas, pearl onions, green beans, cauliflower, sometimes asparagus, artichokes.
Clamart: peas
Crécy: carrots
Doria: cucumbers (cooked in butter)
Dubarry: cauliflower
Fermiére: carrots, turnips, onions, and celery, cut into uniform slices
Florentine: spinach
Forestiére: mushrooms
Judic: braised lettuce
Lyonnaise: onions
Niçoise: tomatoes concassée cooked with garlic
Parmentier: potatoes
Princesse: asparagus
Provençale: tomatoes with garlic, parsley, and sometimes mushrooms and /or olives
Vichy: carrots

Modern hot platter garnish
In classical cuisine, food was nearly always brought to the dining room on large platters and then served, rather than being plated in the kitchen as is most often done today.

Platter of fish Comorian

This practice is still widely used for banquets, and nothing stimulates appetites as much as a succulent roast on a silver platter, sumptuously adorned with a colorful variety of vegetable garnishes.

Decorated grilled rabbit

The classical garnitures most often adapted to modern platter presentation are those called Bouquetière, Jardinière, and Printanière. At one time these are very specific vegetable assortments cut in prescribed ways. But today they are taken in a more general way, meaning colorful assortments of various fresh vegetables. Platter garnish need not be elaborate or difficult to prepare. A simple assortment of colorful vegetables, carefully cut and properly cooked to retain color and texture, is appropriate to the most elegant presentation. Stuffed vegetables, such as tomato halves filled with peas, are a little fancier, but still easy to prepare. Borders of duchesse potatoes are also popular.

Hot dishes in the buffet

Many of the rules of proper plating apply to platter arrangement as well, for example, those that call for neatness, balance of color and shape, unit and preserving the individuality of the items. Following are a few other guidelines that apply to hot platter presentation and garnish. Examples of hot platters are included with the color plates.

Camping Buffet

Arrangements on the matters or glass dinky

Observe the following guidelines when plating food:

1. *Keep food off the rim of the plate*

2. *Arrange the items for the convenience of the customer*
   The meat or other main item should be directly in front, with accompaniments and garnish to the rear and sides. Put the best side of the meat forward. The customer should not have to turn the item around to start on it.   The bony or fatty edge of the steak, the back side of the half duckling, the boniest parts of the chicken pieces, and so on, should face *away* from the customer.

3. Keep space between items

Don't pile everything together in a jumbled heap. Each item should have its own identity. This is of course related also to selecting the right plate size.

4. Maintain unity

Basically, there is unit when the plate looks like one meal that happens to be made up of several items, rather than like several unrelated items that just happen to be on the same plate. Create a center of attention and relate everything to it. The meat is generally the center of attention and is usually placed front and center. Other items are placed around and behind it so as to balance it and keep your eyes centered rather than pulled off the edge of the plate.

5. Make the garnish count

Garnishes are added not just for color. Sometimes they are needed to balance out a plate by provided an additional element. Two items on a plate often look unbalanced, but adding a garnish completes the picture. On the other hand, don't add unnecessary garnishes. Often the food is attractive and colorful without garnish, and adding it clutters the plate and increases your food cost as well.

6. Keep it simple

As you have heard before, simplicity is more attractive than overworked, contrived arrangements or complicated designs. Unusual patterns are occasionally very effective, but avoid making the food look to cute or too elaborate. One of the simplest plating styles can also be one of the most attractive if it is carefully done that is, placing only the meat or fish item and its sauce, if any in the center of the plate. Vegetable accompaniments are then served in separate dishes. This method is widely used in restaurants to simplify service in the kitchen. However, it is usually best to use this method for only some of the menu items, in order to avoid monotony.

Temperature
Serve hot foods hot, on hot plates
Serve cold foods cold, on cold plates
Your arrangement of beautiful food will not make much of a final impression if you
forget this rule.

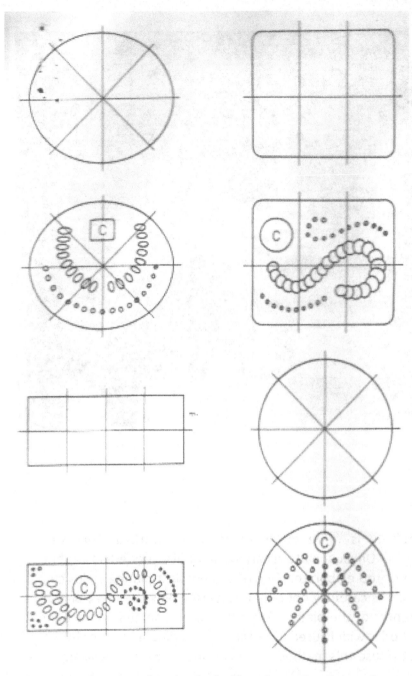

Begin your planning sketch of a buffet platter by diving the tray into six or eight sections This shape you lay out a balanced symmetrical design
The example shown there indicate the placement of the main item
(Usually slice of foods,) of the centerpiece (labeled 'c'), and of the
garnish shows as tiny circles)

Curves and angles are said to have movement. Square corners do not.

Give the design of a focal point

This is the function of the centerpiece, which emphasizes and strengthens the design by giving it direction and height. This may be done very directly, by having the lines point directly to it, or more subtly by having them angle toward it or sweep around it in graceful curves.

Note that the centerpiece isn't always in the center , in spite of its name. Because of its height, it should be at the back or toward the side, so it doesn't hide the food. Remember, you are designing the platter from the customer's point of view.

An example of a buffet display layout

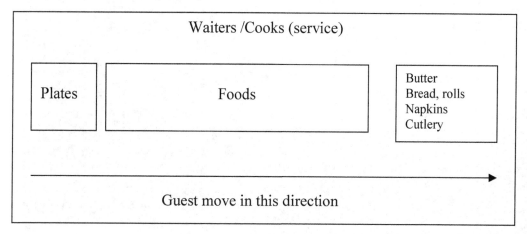

Arranging rows of foods in curves or in angled lines gives movement the design

It is not necessary for every platter on the buffet to have a centerpiece. Some of them should, however, or the buffet will lack height and be less interesting to the eye.

Keep items in proportion

The main items on the platter – the slices of meat, pâté or whatever – should look like the main items. The centerpiece should not be so larger or so tall that it totally dominates the platter. The garnish should enhance, not overwhelm the main item in size, height, or quantity. The number of portions of garnish should be in proportion to the amount of the main item. The size of the platter should be in proportion to the amount of food. Don't select one that is so small as to become crowded or so large as to look almost empty even before the first guest has arrived. Keep enough space between items or between rows so that the platter doesn't look jumbled or confused.

Let the guest see the best side of everything
Angle overlapping slices and wedge-shaped pieces toward the customer, and make sure that the best side of each slice is face up.

Cheese platters
Cheese trays are popular on both luncheon buffets as a main course item and on dinner buffets as a dessert item. Cheeses are presented much differently from the other cold buffet foods we have been talking about. First, whole cheeses or cheeses in large pieces are generally more attractive than arrangements of slices. This also helps the guest identify the varieties. Be sure to supply several knives, so guests can cut their own portions. Second, an assortment of fresh fruit is often included on a cheese tray. It adds a great deal to the appearance of a cheese presentation, and its flavors go well with cheese. An example of a cheese and fruit platter

Sanitation
Cold food for buffets presents a special sanitation problem.

One type of cheese and fruit platter for buffet

This is because the food spends a great deal of time out of refrigeration while it is being assembled and decorated and again while it sits o the buffet. For this reason it is particularly important to follow all the rules of safe food handling. Keep foods refrigerated whenever they are not being worked on. Also keep them chilled until the last minute before they are to be brought out for service. For a buffet service that lasts a long time, it is a good idea to make each course or item on a number of smaller platters rather than on one big one. The replacements can then be kept refrigerated until needed.

Hot Foods for Buffets
Everything we have learned about the preparation and holding of hot foods in quantity applies to hot foods for buffets. Hot items are nearly always served from chafing dishes, which may be ornate silver affairs or simple steam table pans kept warm over hot water. These foods cannot be elaborately decorated and garnished the way cold foods can. On the other hand, the bright, fresh, juicy appearance and good aroma of properly cooked hot food is generally sufficient to arouse appetites.

Hot foods for chafing dishes should be easily portioned (such as vegetables served with a kitchen spoon) or already portioned in the pan (braised pork chops, sliced baked ham, and poached fish fillets, for example). Items not suitable for buffets are those which must be cooked to order and served immediately, such as most broiled or deep fried foods. Whole roasts are popular items at buffets, carved to order by a member of the kitchen staff. Especially attractive are large roasts such as hams, turkeys and large cuts of beef such as steamship round. As we have said, hot foods are best placed at the end of the buffet, so that they will not cool off on the guests' plates before they are seated, so that the decorated cold foods can steal the show.

Tables and chairs setting scene

The Importance of Appearance

We eat for enjoyment as well as for nutrition and sustenance. Cooking is not just a trade but an art that appeals to our senses of taste, smell, and sight. "The eye eats first" is a well known maximum. Out first impressions of a plate of food set our expectations. The sight of food stimulates our appetites, starts our digestive juices flowing, and makes us eager to "dig in" our meal becomes exciting and stimulating. On the other hand, if the food looks carelessly served, tossed onto the plate in a sloppy manner, we assume it was cooked with the same lack of care. If the colors are pale and washed out, with no color accent, we expect the flavors to be bland and monotonous. If the size of the plate makes the steak look small (even if it's not), we go away unsatisfied. You job as cooks and chefs then is to get your customer interested in your food or, better yet, excited about it. You can't afford to turn them off before they even taste it. Your success depends upon making your customers happy.

Making food look good requires first of all that you use proper cooking techniques. If a fish is overcooked and dry or a green vegetable is drab and mushy, it won't look good no matter what you do with it. Second, serving attractive food is largely matter of being neat and careful and using common sense is an aspect of the professionalism we discussed in professionals take pride in their work and in the food they serve. They don't put up a plate with sauce dribbled all over the rim and may be a thumb print or two for extra effect not because their supervisors told them not to or because a rule in a textbook says "don't dribble sauce all over the rim of the plate," but because it's not professional. Third, beyond just being neat, effective food presentation depends upon developing an understanding of techniques involving balance, arrangement, and garniture. These are the subjects of our next sections.

Fundamentals of Plating

We've said before that a plate of food is like a picture, and the rim of the plate is the frame. This does not mean that you have to spend as much time arranging the plate as Rembrandt did painting a portrait, but it.

Cold Meat Dishes – Plats de viandes froides

These refer to cold dishes made from *meat, poultry and game*. Although they are often combined and prepared with jelly, pickles, and salads, they can also be served individually. The primary forms of preparation are roasting, braising, and poele

Beef – Boeuf

Fillet, roast sirloin of beef, rib steak, rump pot roast
Roast to desired degree of doneness. Use simple decorations for whole pieces and coat with a thin layer of jelly. Accompaniments: spring vegetables, tomatoes, asparagus, spears, pickles, shaped mushrooms, fruit, jelly cubes, and parsley. Sauces: variations of mayonnaise, cold Horseradish sauce, cream cheese sauce with Roquefort.

Tongue – langue: Boil, trim, dress, and cool: Use simple decorations and coat with a thin layer of jelly. Accompaniment: same as fillet but without fruits. Sauce: Horseradish Sauce and cream cheese sauce with herbs.

Veal – Veau

Saddle, breast, fillet, filet mignon, loin, rump, round of beef
Whole pieces should be decorated simply and coated with a thin layer of jelly. Accompaniments that may be used with these meats are: vegetables a la grecque, tomatoes, stuffed artichoke hearts, asparagus spears, vegetable salad, mushrooms, fruit only as decoration. Sauces: variations of mayonnaise, cold Horseradish sauce, and cream cheese sauce with herbs.

Always check every now and then if something is needed

Pork – Porc

Loin of pork, ham; Roast or glaze a loin, Simmer or braise a ham depending upon the type of dish. Use simple decorations for whole pieces and coat with a thin layer of jelly. Accompaniments: sweet glazed vegetables, such as carrots, turnips, fruit, such as mustard fruit, stewed apples, and prunes. Sauces: apples puree, cold Horseradish Sauce, or Cranberry Sauce.

Lamb - Agneau
Baron, saddle, roast breast leg; Roast the meat until rare. Use simple decorations for whole pieces and coat with a thin layer of jelly. Accompaniments: mixed pickles, vegetables a la grecque and those mentioned with veal. Sauce: Mint Sauce or cold Horseradish Sauce.

Poultry – Volaille
Poularde, duck, goose, turkey Roast or poele Decorate according to the type of dish, coat with jelly or with Chaud-froid Sauce Accompaniments for duck and turkey: stewed apples, oranges, sweet and sour fruits, glazed chestnuts, and spring vegetables. Accompaniments for poularde: spring vegetables coated with jelly mushrooms, tomatoes, asparagus spears, and artichokes. Sauces for duck, goose, and turkey: Cranberry, Cumberland, and cold Horseradish Sauce.

Sauce for poulardes: variations of Mayonnaise or Cream Cheese Sauce with herbs.

Bar should always be nearby

Game – Gibier

Woodcock, quail, grouse, pheasant, partridge, saddle and leg of roebuck, boar, saddle of hare Roast the meat until rare. Depending on the dish, decorate coat with jelly or with Chaud – froid sauce. Accompaniment: stuffed apples and pears, pineapple, red cherries, oranges, mustard fruit, mixed pickles, spring vegetables a la grecque. Sauces: Cumberland, Cranberry, Horseradish, and Cream cheese with ginger.

Starters

Special Variations

Cold Boiled, Southern France Style – Boeuf Bouilli froid a la mode du Midi.
Boil a beef rump and allow to cool. Slice and garnish on one side with spring vegetables a la grecque and on the other side with stuffed tomatoes and cucumbers. Serve cold horseradish sauce and whipped cream cheese with herbs separately.

Cold braised beef- boeuf a la mode froid. This dish has been handed down from the old French cuisine. Lard a beef rump roast and braise with calf's feet and vegetables but do not bind the gravy with flour coat an appropriate mold with jelly, garnish with the braised vegetables, and fix these with a second layer of jelly. Place the braised beef in the mold and fill it with the gravy. When cold turn out and garnish.

Cold beef Tenderloin with Asparagus spears – filet de boeuf froid Argenteuli
Roast the whole tenderloin and glaze. Arrange on a dish, carve a few slices, garnish with asparagus spears, and coat with jelly

Beef Tenderloin Chevet – fillet de boeuf Chevet. Coat a cradle – shaped mold with jelly, line with various colored, shaped, and well seasoned vegetables, and fix these with another layer of jelly. Place the roast tenderloin in the mold and fill the mold with jelly. Refrigerate until congealed; unmold and garnish.

Cold beef tenderloin with spring vegetables – filet de boeuf froid a la printaniere.

Roast he whole tenderloin and glaze. Arrange on a dish, surround with blanched and marinated spring vegetables which are coated with jelly.

Cold roast beef – roastbeef froid. Roast the whole piece and glaze. Arrange on a dish, carve a few slices, and place them in front of the roast. Garnish the meat with vegetable salad and coat with jelly.

Duck with tongue – caneton a l'ecarlate. Poeler a duck and cool in the stock. Remove the two breast pieces and the skin, slice the breast meat, and rearrange on the breastbone with a half slice of orange between each slice of meat. Surround the bird with medallions of beef tongue alternating with glazed orange slices. Serve cold Horseradish Sauce separately.

Ham souffle Marguerite – Jambon Souffle Marguerite Simmer a smoked ham slowly and cool in the stock. Remove the top part horizontally along the bone. Prepare a mousse with this meat and arrange on the cut surface. Cover with slices of ham and cornets. Accompaniments: ham rolls, stuffed tomatoes, and stuffed green sweet peppers, all thinly coated with jelly. Sauce: Horseradish Sauce.

Breasts of Poularde, Hawaiian Style – supremes de poularde Hawaii Slice the breasts of 2 roast poulardes lengthwise. Place 2 pineapple halves cut lengthwise and hollowed out, in the center of a platter and garnish with celery salad and slices of pineapple and banana. Arrange a sliced breast half in a fan shape on each side of the two pineapples halved. Surround with small goose liver medallions garnished with truffle slices. Coat the whole dish with a thin layer of aspic. Serve Cumberland sauce separately.

Supremes de dinde au jambon saumone et truffles. Roast the turkey breasts, slice, and arrange in the original order with slices of truffles. Stuff a pineapple with celery salad and diced pineapple and surround with ham rolls stuffed with celery salad, and truffle croquettes. The truffles should be served in their natural shape.

Examples of buffet menus for display

Gala Buffet

Various Shellfish
Cold Salmon
Shrimp with Avocados
Cold Turbot Joinville
Zurish Stuffed Pike
Danish Stuffed Eel
Swedish Salmon
Rolls of Sole Rosita

Double Consomme with Sherry

Pate Maison
Roast Beef Nicoise
Fillet of Beef Wellington
Saddle of Veal with Garden Vegetables
Terrins with Calvados
Saddle of Venison Diana
Turkey Mexican Style
Veal and Ham Pie
Pheasant Bristol
Beef Tongue a l'escarlate

Variety of Salads

Boiled Beef Cultivateur
Country Ham in a Crust

Cold Buffet

Melon – Grapefruit – Tomato juice

Terrine of Caviar Malossol

Consome in a Madrilene Cup

Poached Eggs with Tarragon
Medallions of Crawfish, Parisian Style
Norwegian Salmon
Fillets of Sole Calypso

Ham a la Gelee
Roast Beef with Spring Vegetables
Veal Tongue Argenteuil
Mousse de Foie Gras with Paprika

Pate of Chicken with Truffles
Chicken Vendome
Chaud –froid Pheasant
Qual Glace

Russian Salad – Hearts of Lettuce

Fruit Salad with Kirsch
Coupe Melba

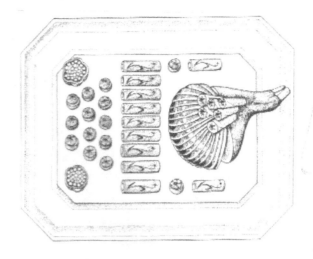

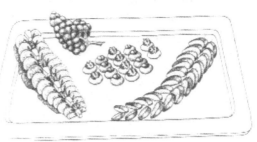

Saddle of dear with fruit – selle de chevreuil aux fruits

Ham souffle marguerite – Jambon Souffle marguerite

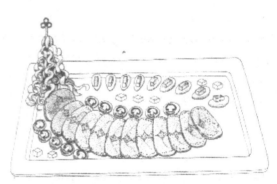

Suckling pig, modern style –cochon de lait

Saddle of veal, bohemian style – selle de

Veal Cutlets with Ham Mousse – *cotes de veau a la mousse de jambon.* Decorate the grilled cold cutlets and coat with jelly. Invert ham mousse in the center of a platter and surround with the cutlets. Garnish with jelly cubes. Serve Horseradish Sauce separately.

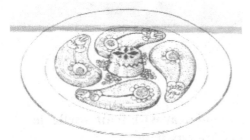

**Veal de cutlets with ham mousse –
cotes de veau a la mousse**

Saddle of Veal, Bohemian Style – *Selle de veau boheme* Stuff a roasted, boned saddle of veal with stuffing mixed with pistachios and red sweet peppers. Tie, coat with jelly, cool, slice, and arrange on a dish. *Accompaniments:* artichoke hearts stuffed with beans, tomatoes and mushrooms and thin slices of hard-cooked eggs with jelly. An elegant decoration consists of round truffles on a spit with garlands of raw carrots, cucumbers, and radishes.

Leg of Venison in Pastry, Lucerne Style – *Gigot de chevreuil en a la lucernoise*

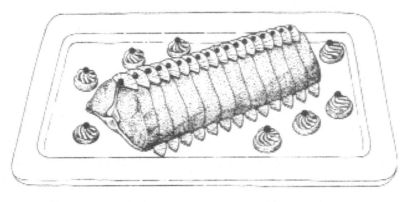

Cold Saddle of Venison St. Hubert – *Selle de chevreuli froid St. Hubert*

Roast a saddle of venison and allow to cool. Remove the fillets and cut into inform slices. Spread some game mousse (mousse de gibier) over the backbone, replace the slices in their original order, and coat with game mousse to give a smooth surface. Place thin, halved pineapple slices along the top of the backbone and decorate with cherries. Garnish bot sides of the saddle with quartered pineapple slices. Arrange some game mousse on poached slices of apple and place a red cherry on top of each. Coat the whole dish with jelly. Serve a Cumberland sauce and Waldorf sauce separately.

Practical performance Assessment
Direct Performance

Performance Criteria	Direct Performance	Assessment		
		I	II	III
The trainee must be able to prepare and display buffet.	1. Collect ingredients. 2. Do mis-en-place 3. Cook foods for hot and cold buffet display. 4. Arrange foods on platters of food warmer containers. 5. Lay out a buffet table for display of food items. 6. Display hot or cold dishes on the buffet tables. 7. Garnish according to start rules on garnishes.			

Product Assessment

Product Specification	Assessment		
	Acceptable	Needs for the Adjustments	Not Acceptable
1. The menu was planned gastronomically			
2. The dishes were (i). Fresh (ii). Delicious (iii). Presentable			
3. The display of the buffet was formidable (i). Appetizing (ii). Color contrast showing			

Knowledge Assessment

ORAL QUESTIONS	WRITTEN QUESTIONS
Question the trainee while performing the taste 1. When he/she is preparing the dish warmers. 2. Hygiene questions	1. Write down in your own words what is buffet. 2. Compose one acceptable menu of marriage reception. 3. What are the 12 different dishes which can be displayed in the buffet? 4. When you are preparing a cold buffet platter, why is it a good idea to plan ahead by making a sketch? What would you include in the sketch? 5. What do the terms movement and focal point mean in platter design?

Chapter 5

KITCHEN ORGANISATION, STAFFING, DESIGN ING AND KITCHEN EQUIPMENTS

KITCHEN EQUIPMENTS

Kitchen Organization, Staffing, Designing and Kitchen Equipments

Kitchen Equipments

Objectives	The trainee should be able to identify and use all equipment in the kitchen after completing this unit
Duration	
Equipment / tools	Equipment of the kitchen
Training Materials	PICTURES
Teaching Aid	HAND OUTS
Reference Materials	ELEMENTARY SCIENCE OF FOOD E.M HILDRETH FOOD AND NUTRITION - ANITAL TULL
Trainee Preparation:	Discuss with the trainee about all the large equipment and how they function

Kitchen Organization, Staffing, Designing and Kitchen Equipments

Kitchen Equipments

Duration	Instruction Steps	Illustration
	To start with the trainee should know: 1. Introduction to catering equipment 2. Stoves and how to keep them 3. Convection ovens and how they operate 4. Microwave ovens and their operations 5. Induction cookers and its energy 6. Halogen Hob 7. Steamers 8. Brat pan 9. Boiling pans	

Kitchen Organization, Staffing, Designing and Kitchen Equipments

Kitchen Equipments

CETERING EQUIPMENT

Introduction

Kitchen equipment is expensive so initial selection is important, and the following point should be considered before each item purchased or hired:

Overall dimensions – in relation to available space
Weight – can the floor support the weight?
Fuel supply – is the existing fuel supply sufficient to take the increase?
Drainage – were necessary, are there adequate facilities?
Water – where necessary, is it to hand?
Use – does the food to be provided justify good use?
Capacity can it cooks the quantities of food required efficiently?
Time – Can it cook the quantities of food in the time available?
Ease – Is it easy for staff to handle, control and use properly?
Maintenance – is it easy for staff to clean and maintain?
Attachment – is it necessary to use additional equipment or attachments?
Extraction – Does it require attraction facility for fumes or steam?
Noise – does it have acceptable noise level?
   Construction – is it well made and is all handles, knobs and switches sturdy and heat resistance?

Spare parts – are they and replacement easily obtainable?

Kitchen equipment may be divided into three categories:
1. Large equipment – ranges, streamers, boiling pans, fish-flyers, sinks, tables, etc.
2. Mechanical equipment – peelers, mincers, mixers, refrigerator, and dish washers etc.
3. Utensils and small equipment – ports, pans, whisks, bowls, spoons, etc.

Manufactures of large mechanical kitchen equipment issue instructions on how to keep their apparatus in efficient working order, and it is the responsibility of every one using the equipment to follow these instructions

(Which should be displayed in prominent place near the machinery?)

Arrangement should be made with the local gas board for regular checks and saving of gas – operated equipment; similar arrangements should be made with the electricity supplier. It is good plan to keep a log – book of all equipment, showing where each item is located when servicing takes place, noting any defects that arise, and instructing the fitter to sing the log-book and to indicate exactly what has been done.

Large Equipment

Stoves

A large variety of stoves is available operated by gas, electricity, solid fuel, oil, microwave or microwave plus convection. Sold tops should be washed or wiped clean with a pad sacking. When cool, the stovetops can be more thoroughly cleaned by washing and using an abrasive. After any kind of cleaning a sold top should always be lightly greased.

On the open type of stove all the bars and racks should be removed, immersed in hot water with detergent, scrubbed clean, dried and put back place o the stove. The gas jets should then be lit to check that none are blocked. All enamel parts of stoves should be cleaned while wormed with hot detergent water, rinsed and dried.

The inside of the ovens and oven racks should be cleaned while slightly warm, using detergent water and mild abrasive if necessary. In cases of extreme dirty or grease being backed on to the stove or oven caustic jelly may be used, but through rinsing must take place after wards.

Oven doors should not be slammed, as this is liable to cause damage.
The unnecessary or premature lighting of ovens can cause wastage of fuel, which is needless expense. This is a bad habit common in many kitchens. When a sold –top gas is range is lit, the center ring should be removed, but it should be replaced after approximately 5 minutes, otherwise unnecessary heat is lost.

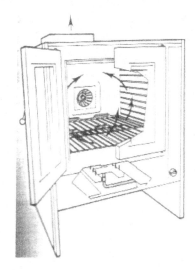

Convection ovens

These are ovens in which a circulating current of hot air is rapidly forced around the inside of the oven by motorized fan or blower. As a result, a more even and contact temperature is created which h allows food to be cooked sufficient in any part of oven. This means that the heat is used more efficiently, cooking temperatures can be lower, cooking times shortened and overall fuel economy archived.

Forced air convection can be described as fact conventional cooking; conventional in that heat is applied to the surface of food, but fast since moving air transfers its heat more rapidly than does static air. In a sealed oven, fast hot air circulation reduced evaporation loss, keeping shrinkage to a minimum, and gives the rapid change of surface texture and color which are traditionally associated with certain cooking process

There are four types of convection oven:

1. When forced air circulation within the oven is accomplished by means of a motor –driven fan, the rapid air circulation ensures even temperature distribution to all parts of oven

2. Where low velocity, high volume air movement is provided by a power blower and duct system.

3. A combination of standard oven and forced convention oven designed to operate as either by the flick or as switch.

4. A Single roll – in rack convection oven with heating element and fan housed outside the cooking area. An 18 –shelf mobile oven rack make it possible to roll the filled rack direct from the preparation area into the oven.

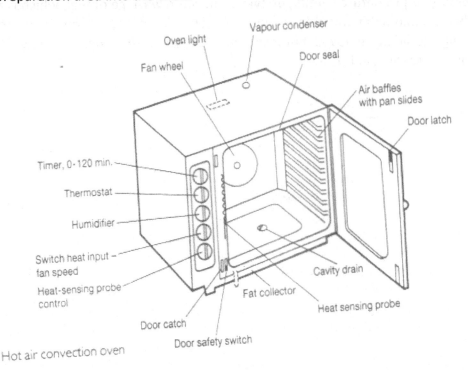

Hot air convection oven

Convection and steaming oven

This combination oven can be used for cooking by convection, stream or a combination of both. It can be used for roasting, braising, poaching, fast streaming, backing grilling, toasting, defrosting, and re generating frozen and cook-chill foods.

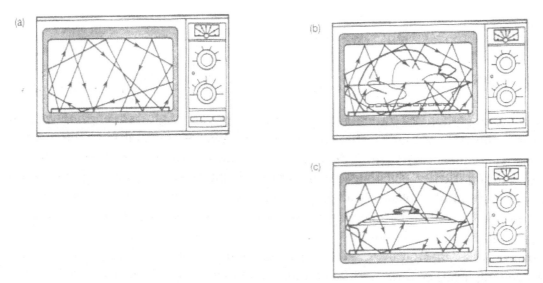

(a) Microwave energy being refracted off cooking cavity walls, (b) microwave energy being absorbed by food, (c) microwave energy passing through cooking container material

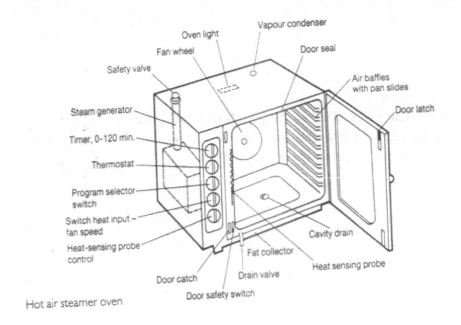

Hot air steamer oven

Microwave Ovens

Microwave is the method of cooking and heating food by using high frequency power. The energy used is the same as that which carries television from the transmitter to the receiver, but is at higher frequency. The waves disturb the molecules or particles of food and agitate them, thus causing friction which has the effect of cooking the whole of the food. In the conventional method of cooking, heat penetrated the food only by conduction from the outside. Food being cooked by microwave need to fat or water, and is placed in a glass, earthenware, plastic or paper container before being put in the oven. Metal is not used as the microwaves are reflected by it. All microwave ovens consist of a basic unit of various sizes with varying levels of power. Some feature additions to the standard model, such as automatic defrosting systems, browning elements, 'stay-hot' controls and revolving turntables.

The oven cavity has metallic walls, ceiling and floor which reflect the microwaves. The oven door is fitted with special seals to ensure that there is minimum microwave leakage. A cut-out device automatically switches off the microwave energy when the door is opened. When cleaning, do not allow the cleaning agent to soil or accumulate around the door seal as this could prevent a tight seal when the door is closed. Never use an abrasive cleaner to clean the interior of the oven as it can internal parts of the oven. Follow the manufacturer's instructions carefully for cleaning.

Combination convection and microwave cooker

This cooker combines forced air convection and microwave, either of which can be used separately but which are normally used simultaneously, thereby giving the advantages of both systems: speed, coloration and texture of food. Traditional metal cooking pans may also be used without fear of damage to the cooker.

Induction cookers

These are sold top plates made of vitro-ceramic material which provide heat only when pans are put on them and which stop the heat immediately the pans are removed. A generator creates a two-way magnetic field at the top level. When a utensil with a magnetic base is placed on the top a current passes directly to the pan, conventional cooking equipment. Since the ceramic top is not magnetic but merely a tray to stand the pots and pans on, it never heats up. Tests indicate more than 50 per cent energy saving. If a pan of water is to be brought to the boil there is no delay waiting for the top to heat up; the transmission of energy through the pan is immediate. When shallow frying, cold oil and the food can be put into the pan together without affecting the quality of the food as the speed of heating is so rapid.

Induction tops have a number of advantages over ranges using conventional sources:

Energy saving   faster cooking time

            hygienic

Flexible   easy maintenance   safe

Improved working environment (less heat in the kitchen)

However, induction tops are expensive and special cooking utensils are required. Any non-magnetic material does not work and aluminum and copper are unsuitable. Stainless steel, enameled ware, iron and specially adapted copper pans are suitable.

The halogen hob

This runs on electricity, and comprises five individually controlled heat zones, each of which has four tungsten halogen lamps located under a smooth ceramic glass surface. The heat source glows red, when switched on, getting brighter as the temperature increases. When the hob is switched on, 70 per cent of the heat is transmitted as infra-red light directly into the base of the cooking pan; the rest is from conducted heat via the ceramic glass. Ordinary pots and pans may be used on the halogen hob. The halogen range includes a convection oven, and the halogen hob unit is also available mounted on a stand.

Steamers

There are basically three types of steaming ovens:
(a) Atmospheric
(b) Pressure
(c) Pressure less.

There are also combination steaming ovens, e.g. pressure/convection steam;

Pressure less /full pressurized; steaming /hot air cooking; combination of hot air and steam; combination of hot air and steam with two settings. In addition, dual pressure steamers, switchable between low pressure and high pressure, and two pressure settings plus zero are available. Steaming ovens continue to develop, improve and become more versatile. The modern combination steamer can be selected for steaming, stewing, poaching, braising, roasting, grilling, baking, vacuum cooking, gratinating, toasting, reconstituting, blanching and defrosting. With such a wide range of models available it is increasingly important available it is increasingly important to consider carefully which model is best suited to a particular kitchen's requirements.

Cleanliness of steamers is essential, and trays and runner should be washed in hot detergent water and then rinsed. Any water generating chamber should be drained, cleaned and refilled and the inside of the steamer cleaned. Grease door controls occasionally, and when the steamer is not in use, leave the door slightly open to let air circulate inside the steam

Brat pan

The brat pan is one of the most versatile pieces of cooking equipment in the kitchen because it is possible to use it for shallow frying, deep-frying, stewing, braising and boiling. A brat pan can cook many items of food at one time because of its large surface

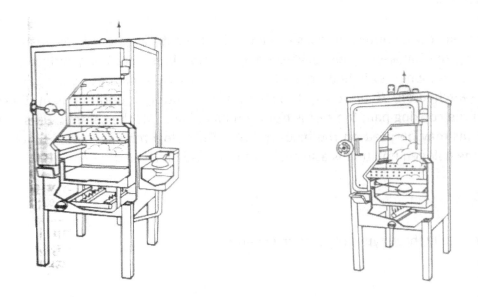

Fig. 10.7 *Atmospheric steamers*

area. A further advantage is that it can be tilted so that the contents can be quickly and efficiently poured out on completion of the cooking process. Brat pans are heated by gas or electricity and several models are available incorporating various features to meet differing catering requirements.

Boiling pans Many types are available in different metals aluminum, stainless steel, etc- in various sizes (10, 15, 20, 30 and 40 liter capacity) and the may be heated by gas or electricity. As they are used for boiling or stewing large quantities of food it is important that they do not allow the food to burn; for this reason the steam-jacket type boiler is the most suitable. Many of these are fitted with a tilting device to facilitate the emptying of the contents. After use, the boiling pan and lid should be thoroughly washed with mild detergent solution and then well rinsed. The tilting apparatus should be greased occasionally and checked to see that it tilts easily. If gas fired, the gas jets and pilot should be inspected to ensure correct working. If a pressure gauge and safety valve are fitted these should also be checked.

Practical performance Assessment
Direct Performance

Performance Criteria	Direct Performance	Assessment		
		I	II	III
The trainee should know how to:- 1. Take care of the stove 2. Operate ovens 3. Operations of microwave 4. How to use cookers 5. Steamers 6. Brat pan 7. Boiling pans.	• Clean the stove operates the oven. • Operate microwave • Using of cookers putting on and switching off of steamers brat pan boiling pans.			

Product Assessment

Product Specification	Assessment		
	Acceptable	Needs for the Adjustments	Not Acceptable
1. The stove was clean and filled accordingly.			
2. The oven was switched on and switched off without any incident.			
3. The micro oven was switched on and the trainee could operate it in all spheres.			
4. The trainee did put on the steamers • Brat pan • Boiling pans			
5. He /she observed the safety regulations.			

Knowledge Assessment

ORAL QUESTIONS	WRITTEN QUESTIONS
Ask question when performing the task (i). Safety precautions when switching on the machines. (ii). Safety precautions when putting water in the machines.	1. How many types of convection ovens can you get? 2. What is convection and steaming over? 3. Describe how micro oven operates.

CPSIA information can be obtained
at www.ICGtesting.com
Printed in the USA
LVOW03s1556250216

476702LV00011B/481/P

9 781506 196312